Female FOODIES

Marie Callender

Homemade Pie Maven

Rebecca Felix

Checkerboard Library

An Imprint of Abdo Publishing
abdopublishing.com

abdopublishing.com

Published by Abdo Publishing, a division of ABDO, PO Box 398166, Minneapolis, Minnesota 55439. Copyright © 2018 by Abdo Consulting Group, Inc. International copyrights reserved in all countries. No part of this book may be reproduced in any form without written permission from the publisher. Checkerboard Library™ is a trademark and logo of Abdo Publishing.

Printed in the United States of America, North Mankato, Minnesota
102017
012018

Design: Sarah DeYoung, Mighty Media, Inc.
Production: Mighty Media, Inc.
Editor: Liz Salzmann
Cover Photographs: Mighty Media, Inc.
Interior Photographs: Alamy, pp. 5, 15, 17, 25; Getty Images, p. 27; iStockphoto, p. 9; Photo courtesy Orange County Archives, pp. 11, 28 (top); Roadsidepictures/Flickr, pp. 13, 28 (bottom); Shutterstock, pp. 7, 21, 23, 29
Background Pattern: Shutterstock, cover, pp. 3, 5, 7, 9, 11, 13, 15, 17, 21, 23, 25, 27, 31

MARIE CALLENDER'S® is a registered trademark of ConAgra Foods RDM, Inc., used with permission.

Publisher's Cataloging-in-Publication Data
Names: Felix, Rebecca, author.
Title: Marie Callender: homemade pie maven / by Rebecca Felix.
Other titles: Homemade pie maven
Description: Minneapolis, Minnesota : Abdo Publishing, 2018. | Series: Female foodies |
    Includes online resources and index.
Identifiers: LCCN 2017944038 | ISBN 9781532112652 (lib.bdg.) | ISBN 9781532150371 (ebook)
Subjects: LCSH: Callender, Marie, 1907-1995.--Juvenile literature. | Businesswomen--United States--
    Biography--Juvenile literature. | Pies--Juvenile literature. | Entrepreneurship--Juvenile literature.
Classification: DDC 338.76647 [B]--dc23
LC record available at https://lccn.loc.gov/2017944038

Contents

Chapter 1

Pie Icon

You're at home and hungry for a hearty meal. But you have to leave for your piano lesson in 20 minutes! Luckily, there's a Marie Callender's turkey dinner in the freezer. You open the square, green box and pop the dinner in the microwave oven. Your meal is ready in no time! You top it off with a boxed dessert inspired by Callender's famous pies.

The name Marie Callender's is well-known around the country as a brand of frozen meals and desserts. But Marie Callender's is also a **chain** of restaurants. These eateries got their start when the woman they were named after became renowned for her homemade pies.

Marie Callender was born in 1907 in South Dakota. Little is known about her early life and family, including her last name. In the 1920s, Marie's family moved west to California. There, Marie met and married Cal Callender in 1924.

Food Bite

Both Marie and Cal were only 17 years old when they married!

Today, there
are more than
65 Marie
Callender's
restaurants.

In 1928, Callender gave birth to her and Cal's only son,
Don. Callender spent much of the next 20 years raising
Don and managing the family's household. In the 1940s,
Callender's life changed when she decided to begin a career.

Chapter 2

Baking Boom

Callender had become a skilled baker and cook while taking care of her family. In the 1940s, she decided to put these skills to work outside the home. Callender took a part-time job at a delicatessen. There, she made salads and hot foods.

Soon, the delicatessen's owner asked Callender to make pies. She baked the pies at home, using her own recipes. Then she brought the pies to the delicatessen. Customers loved the pies' light, flaky crusts and fresh fruit or cream fillings. The desserts were soon very popular.

Callender's boss encouraged Callender to make more and more pies to meet his customers' demand. He even bought a small bakery where Callender could bake the pies. At the bakery, Callender was able to bake more pies than ever. One day, she baked more than 100 pies by herself!

The demand for Callender's pies continued to grow. Soon, she could not keep up on her own. Callender spoke with her son and husband about helping her. The Callenders decided to turn making pies into a family business.

Callender's pie flavors include banana cream, lemon meringue, key lime, and chocolate satin.

Chapter 3

Setting Up Shop

Callender also spoke with her boss about how busy she had become baking pies. He supported her decision to quit her job to focus on making pies full time. And he promised to buy pies from her for his restaurant. He even let Callender take the oven from his bakery to use in her new business.

With the oven and help from Cal and Don, Callender was ready to get to work. She planned to sell hundreds of pies to local restaurants each week. But making that many pies would require a bigger space than the Callenders' home kitchen.

The Callenders sold the family car. They used the money to fund the business. They rented a Quonset hut in Long Beach, California. The family also purchased baking equipment and supplies.

By 1948, the family business was underway. Callender made the pies. Cal handled the business paperwork. Don handled **marketing** and sales. He worked to establish pie orders from local eateries. Several restaurants and bakeries

Quonset huts were metal buildings originally used by the US military. They had many purposes, including living quarters, offices, storage, and kitchens.

became customers. Callender often baked pies all day and into the night to fill orders. Soon, the small business was producing more than 200 pies a day!

Chapter 4

First Restaurant

The Callenders' success continued for the next 16 years. By then, they were baking thousands of pies each week. They made enough profit to buy better equipment. This included a commercial mixer that could mix the ingredients for many pies at once. The family also bought a new truck for delivering the pies to stores.

Don encouraged his parents to build on their success. He wanted to open a coffee and pie shop to sell pies directly to customers. In 1964, the Callenders opened the first Marie Callender's Pie Shop in Orange, California. The small shop had a working pie oven in its front window. This let customers and people walking by see the pies being baked.

Each new customer received free coffee and a slice of pie on their first visit. The shop stayed busy with both new and repeat customers coming in for Callender's cooking. Soon, the Callenders decided to expand the shop's menu to include soups and sandwiches. As the menu grew, so did the business. The small pie shop became the first in a **chain** of successful restaurants. Many of them remain open today.

Orange is a city located in southwest California. It is known for its historic plaza. The city was planned around the plaza in the 1870s.

Chapter 5

Expanding

Don became the driving force behind opening more Marie Callender's locations. The second shop was in La Habra, California. The third was in Anaheim, California. Just one year after the first restaurant had opened, there were more than 26 Marie Callender's locations.

By the late 1960s, there were more than 100 Marie Callender's restaurants across the Southwest! The additional Marie Callender's locations were just as successful as the original pie shop. Altogether, the business was making more than $100 million in sales each year!

Each location offered meals, desserts, and drinks, all served to customers by a waitstaff. The restaurants' menus also expanded. Many of the new items were made from Callender's personal recipes. Don had also become skilled in the kitchen and he helped create several key dishes.

Don also introduced other **innovations**. It was his idea to add salad bars at Marie Callender's locations. Today, having a salad bar where diners make their own salads is common. But this was a new concept at the time.

Marie Callender's locations still serve classic dishes from the original restaurant, including potpies, roasted turkey dinners, and salads.

Marie Callender's restaurants were among the first to try it out. Don also helped Marie Callender's become one of the first restaurants to **franchise**.

Chapter 6

Chapter 6

Traditions

As Callender's business grew, so did her fame. Soon, her name was well-known across the Southwest. It was associated with homemade comfort foods such as corn bread, meat loaf, and chicken dinners. But Callender's dessert pies remained her most famous products.

Callender never shared her pie recipes. And she never worried about competition. She was sure of the flavor and quality of her flaky fruit- or cream-filled pies. Callender believed that any person who tasted her pies would become a repeat customer.

It seems Callender was right. Residents near each new Marie Callender's location soon grew to love her pies. Many families made Callender's pies a tradition at holiday dinners or for special occasions.

Thanksgiving was an especially busy time at Marie Callender's

Food Bite

✕

The **slogan** of Marie Callender's restaurants is "Home Cooked Happiness."

In 2012, one Marie Callender's restaurant had a whole room full of pies that people ordered ahead of time for Thanksgiving.

restaurants. Customers bought thousands of pies considered traditional for this holiday. This included apple and pecan pies. But pumpkin pies were a customer favorite. Some Marie Callender's locations sold as many as 7,000 pumpkin pies around the Thanksgiving holiday!

Chapter 7

New Owners

Marie Callender's restaurants remained successful through the 1970s and 1980s. The restaurant **chain** also continued to grow during this time. About one new restaurant opened each month. There were locations throughout southern California and in neighboring states.

The Callenders, especially Don, remained **involved** in operating their business. Don visited each location from time to time. There, he would make sure the food was high quality. He also checked that his mother's famous pies were being made correctly.

In 1984, Cal died. This was the beginning of the end of the Callender family's ties to the restaurants. Two years later, Don sold the Marie Callender's chain to hotel company Ramada, Inc. At the time, the Marie Callender's chain was making more than $175 million in sales each year.

Callender, along with her family, turned a homemade pie business into a multi-million-dollar company. She spent 20 years taking care of her family and 40 years devoted to her business. Now, it was time to retire.

Each Marie Callender's location features a
display case of pies. Many of these pie flavors
are based on Callender's original recipes.

Chapter 8

Later Life

In the years following the sale of her restaurant **chain**, Callender remained interested in the company. She often ate at Marie Callender's restaurants. Callender also stayed busy with other interests. She lived in Laguna Hills, California, and was very active with local charities there. She took part in religious events through her church. Callender also spent time with her three grandchildren, Glen, Cathe, and Donald Jr.

In the 1990s, Callender developed **cancer**. She died on November 11, 1995. The Marie Callender's chain changed ownership several times after her death. But, throughout these changes, Callender's name remained, as did her most popular dishes.

Food Bite

Throughout her life, Callender continued to have ideas about how to improve the company.

Marie Callender

By the Numbers

9-27

average price in dollars for a whole Marie Callender's restaurant pie today

22

number of years the Callenders owned and operated the restaurant **chain**

26

number of dessert pie flavors on a Marie Callender's menu

166

number of Marie Callender's locations in 1999, during the height of the chain's success

700

price in dollars the Callenders invested to start their family pie-making business in 1948

10,000

number of nationwide Marie Callender's employees in 1999

38,000,000

number of frozen pies sold in the United States in 2014, many of them Marie Callender's brand

Chapter 9

Frozen Foods

By the mid-1990s, the name Marie Callender's had become associated with homemade-style meals and tasty pies. In 1994, Callender's name expanded beyond the restaurant world and into stores. That year, Marie Callender's **licensed** the Marie Callender's brand name to large US food manufacturer Conagra Brands Inc. Conagra planned to sell a line of Marie Callender's brand frozen dinners. In 2010, Conagra acquired the license to **market** Marie Callender's brand frozen dessert pies.

Conagra makes the frozen foods it sells. But the foods are modeled after Marie Callender's dishes. And although Callender wasn't **involved** in the frozen foods, her story is a part of the brand's marketing. The brand's **slogan** is "From my kitchen to yours since 1948." This refers to the year Callender started her pie business.

Food Bite

✕

Besides potpies, the brand makes a variety of other meals, including sweet & sour chicken, lasagna, and macaroni and cheese.

Potpies are some of Marie Callender's most popular frozen meals.

Like other brands of frozen foods, many of Marie Callender's foods can be cooked in a microwave oven. This makes them convenient for those who have busy lifestyles. People can prepare home-style dinners in minutes.

When the frozen foods **debuted**, only a few western states had Marie Callender's restaurants. But the frozen foods were sold in stores nationwide. This exposed people all across the country to the Marie Callender's brand.

Chapter 10

Joining Forces

The popularity of the Marie Callender's frozen foods brand positively influenced the restaurant **chain**. In 1998, the restaurants made more than $300 million for the first time. By 1999, there were Marie Callender's restaurants in states other than California. These included Colorado, Idaho, Utah, and Washington.

Marie Callender's soon became a household name across the nation. People came to expect that a Marie Callender's frozen or restaurant meal would taste homemade. Many people considered Marie Callender's foods to be classic American dishes.

In 2006, the Marie Callender's chain **merged** with another classic American restaurant group. Perkins Family Restaurants began in Ohio in 1958. By 1981, there were Perkins restaurants in 29 US states. The merger between Perkins and Marie Callender's joined two of the country's most popular casual dining chains. Although now owned by the same company, the two restaurant chains kept their original names and menus.

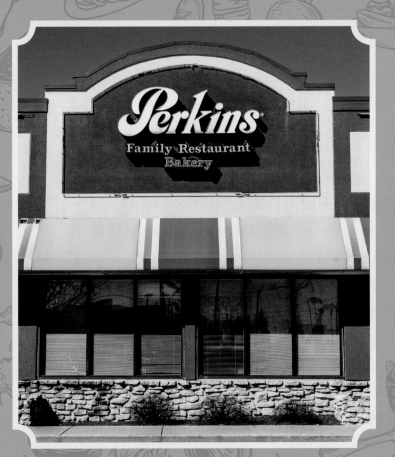

Perkins operates nearly 400 restaurants in the United States and Canada! These include both company-owned restaurants and franchises.

The frozen foods brand remained separately owned. In 2011, Conagra purchased the Marie Callender's brand it had been **licensing**. This gave the food manufacturer greater control of the Marie Callender's brand. Conagra then licensed the Marie Callender's name to the **chain**, allowing restaurants to continue using the name.

Chapter 11

Tough Times

When Marie Callender's **merged** with Perkins in 2006, there were 138 Marie Callender's locations in the United States. However, less than a year later, a **recession** began. The Great Recession was a financial **crisis** that took place worldwide. It lasted until 2009.

During this time, the **economy** declined. Many companies struggled to make a profit. People lost their jobs. Many businesses closed, including in the restaurant industry.

Restaurants providing table service struggled especially. These types of restaurants must pay a waitstaff to serve food. Therefore, the price per dish must be higher than that of competitors without waitstaff. Additionally, diners at restaurants with table service are expected to tip their servers. Many diners did not have extra money during the recession. For these reasons, more people ate

Food Bite

Customer loyalty played a big part in the success of Marie Callender's restaurants and foods.

Perkins and Marie Callender's say one of the main reasons for their success is dedicated, loyal employees.

at restaurants that did not have waitstaff, so they could pay lower prices.

Like many other table service restaurants, Marie Callender's business suffered. In 2011, Marie Callender's and Perkins filed for **bankruptcy**. Thirty-one Marie Callender's restaurants closed. The original location in Orange closed in 2016. By that time, there were about 60 locations left operating across the country.

Chapter 12

Callender's Legacy

From its start in a Quonset hut to becoming a household name, Marie Callender's has had staying power. While some Marie Callender's restaurants closed, the remaining locations are still in operation. These locations serve **signature** items from the original restaurant. This includes the famous pies based on Callender's recipes.

In 1999, restaurant consultant Randall Hiatt credited this success to the reputation Callender built. He said her recipes became famous for providing diners with a home-cooked dining experience. Callender's pies have remained her most famous **legacy**. Fresh or frozen, they are still a popular choice for holidays and family gatherings.

Callender's family values are still a part of the restaurants and foods that bear her name. Restaurant locations provide comfortable, family-friendly settings. And **marketing** for the frozen foods brand aims to bring families together over meals. Callender perfected her skills in her home kitchen. Seventy years later, people are still enjoying foods inspired by her classic homemade creations.

In December 2016, Marie Callender's hosted several holiday dinners in New York City. These events raised money for Habitat for Humanity.

Timeline

1907

Marie is born in South Dakota.

1920s

Marie's family moves to California.

1940s

Callender takes a job at a delicatessen. She begins baking pies at home for the delicatessen.

1948

Callender, Cal, and Don begin a pie-making business out of a Quonset hut in Long Beach, California.

1960s-1970s

Don leads the expansion of Marie Callender's restaurant locations, opening them in several western US states.

1924

Marie marries
Cal Callender.

1928

Marie Callender gives
birth to her son, Don.

1964

The Callenders open
Marie Callender's
Pie Shop in Orange,
California.

1986

The Callenders
sell their
restaurant chain
to Ramada, Inc.

1994

Conagra Foods
starts selling a Marie
Callender's brand of
frozen foods.

1995

Callender dies
from cancer on
November 11.

Glossary

bankruptcy – the state of having been legally declared unable to pay a debt.

cancer – any of a group of often deadly diseases marked by harmful changes in the normal growth of cells. Cancer can spread and destroy healthy tissues and organs.

chain – a group of businesses usually under a single ownership, management, or control.

crisis – a difficult or dangerous situation that needs serious attention.

debut – to make a first appearance.

economy – the way a nation produces and uses goods, services, and natural resources.

franchise – to grant someone the right to sell a company's goods or services in a particular place.

innovation – a new idea, method, or device.

involve – to take part in something.

legacy – something important or meaningful handed down from previous generations or from the past.

license – to allow the use of a name or logo through a formal agreement.

market – to advertise or promote an item for sale. Marketing is the process of advertising or promoting an item for sale.

merge – to combine or blend, such as when two or more companies combine into one business. This process is called a merger.

recession – a period of reduced business activity.

signature – something that sets apart or identifies an individual, group, or company.

slogan – a word or a phrase used to express a position, a stand, or a goal.

Online Resources

Booklinks
NONFICTION NETWORK
FREE! ONLINE NONFICTION RESOURCES

To learn more about Marie Callender, visit **abdobooklinks.com**. These links are routinely monitored and updated to provide the most current information available.

Index